EDGE
BOOKS

BUSTING BOREDOM

IN THE GREAT OUTDOORS

BY TYLER OMOTH

CAPSTONE PRESS
a capstone imprint

Edge Books are published by Capstone Press,
1710 Roe Crest Drive, North Mankato, Minnesota 56003
www.mycapstone.com

Library of Congress Cataloging-in-Publication Data
Cataloging-in-publication information is on file with the Library of Congress.
ISBN 978-1-5157-4703-1 (library binding)
ISBN 978-1-5157-4715-4 (eBook PDF)

Acknowledgements
Alesha Sullivan, editor; Kyle Grenz, designer; Morgan Walters, media researcher;
Katy LaVigne, production specialist; Marcy Morin and Sarah Schuette, project
producers

Photo Credits
Capstone Studio: Karon Dubke, 5, 7, 9, 11, 13, 14, 15, 17, 19, 20, 23, 25, 26,
29; Shutterstock: Bruno Ismael Silva Alves, (grunge texture) design element
throughout, Bryan Solomon, (bottle) Cover, freesoulproduction, (leaves) Cover,
Hein Nouwens, (hammer) Cover, Michele Paccione, (football) Cover, Miguel Angel
Salinas Salinas, (tape) Cover, Nevena Radonja, (camera) Cover, Nikitina Karina,
(string) Cover, PictureStudio, (tape measure) Cover, Slobodan Zivkovic, (leaves)
Cover, vladis.studio, (glue, pen scissors) Cover

Table of Contents

INTO THE WILD

There's nothing on TV. You've conquered all of your video games. You've looked all over the house and nothing looks fun. Now you're bored. What are you going to do?

It's time to get up and bust your boredom in the outdoors! You can build your own games, learn about nature, and practice your sports skills. With a few things that you have around the house and with your imagination, there's no limit to what you can do outside.

Rain or shine—it doesn't matter what the weather is. There are great projects you can work on if you're alone or with friends. When you head outside, you can create your own entertainment. Just follow these simple directions and you'll be having too much fun outdoors to even think about boredom!

SAFETY FIRST

Some of these projects will require adult supervision, while others you'll be able to tackle on your own. Before you begin any project, make sure you have all the required tools and materials, and carefully read all the way through the instructions.

FEED THE BIRDS

MATERIALS

paper towels or newspaper

plastic knife

peanut butter

empty toilet paper tube

birdseed

paper plate

heavy-duty string (optional)

camera (optional)

bird identification book (optional)

Birds need to find a lot of food to survive, especially in winter. This easy-to-make bird feeder is fun, colorful, and sure to bring countless birds outside your window. How many birds can you name?

1 Spread some paper towels or newspaper on an outdoor table.

2 With the plastic knife, spread peanut butter over the outside of the toilet paper tube. Be generous!

3 Pour some birdseed onto the paper plate, covering the surface.

4 Roll the paper tube over the birdseed. Apply some pressure to make sure that the roll is completely covered.

5 Run the string through the toilet paper tube and then tie the ends of the string to a tree branch. Or if you don't have any string, let the feeder sit right on a branch.

6 Step back and wait for the birds to come for a treat! Take pictures if you want or use a bird book to identify the different *species* of birds.

species—a group of plants or animals that share common characteristics

HERE, BIRDY

Different birds like different types of bird feed. Black oil sunflower seeds or shelled sunflower seeds are very popular with cardinals, finches, and nuthatches. Get a bird identification book from the public library or talk to a park ranger to learn more about the birds where you live.

FOOTBALL TARGET TOSS

MATERIALS

large tarp with *grommets* at the corners

yardstick

permanent marker

scissors

colorful duct tape

50 feet (15 meters) of nylon rope

a football, baseball, soccer ball, or other type of ball

Wouldn't it be great if you had a backyard game that would also help you practice your sports skills? Now you do! This football target toss game is easy to make, and it's fun to play alone. Football Target Toss is also easy to fold up and throw in the car to take along on camping trips and vacations. Want to raise the stakes? Invite some friends over and have a competition!

1 Spread the tarp on the ground or a flat surface.

2 Use the yardstick and permanent market to draw four to six different shapes spaced evenly on the tarp. These will become the target holes. They can be squares, triangles, or circles. Make them different sizes so some are easier to hit than others. All of the holes should be large enough to fit the ball through.

grommet—an eyelet placed in a hole of a tarp or panel to protect a rope or cable passing through it or to prevent the tarp or panel from being torn

3 Use the scissors to carefully cut out the shapes.

4 Use duct tape to frame the holes. Fold it over the edge of the hole so it creates a strong border.

5 Use the marker or duct tape to add point values to each hole. Smaller holes are harder to hit, so make them worth more points.

6 Cut the rope into four pieces. Tie a piece of the rope to each corner using the grommet. Hang the tarp from a tree or building.

TIP:
Make sure there is nothing behind the tarp that can be damaged by flying balls.

7 Grab a ball and start tossing! Get together with friends and have a competition. Who can score the most points in five throws?

SIDEWALK CHALK PAINT

MATERIALS

sidewalk chalk (old broken pieces will also work)

plastic bags

hammer

plastic containers with lids

water

paintbrushes of various sizes

Are you feeling artistic? Sidewalk chalk is a fun way to create colorful drawings on the sidewalk or driveway. With this simple project, you can turn sidewalk chalk into paint. Time to get your hands dirty and create your next masterpiece!

1 Sort the pieces of sidewalk chalk by color. Put each color into its own plastic bag.

2 Using the hammer, carefully pound the chalk through the bag until it is powdery.

3 Empty each bag of powder into its own plastic container.

4 Add 1 cup (240 milliliters) water to each container. Put the cover on and shake the container *vigorously*.

5 Take the new paint outside, grab a paintbrush, and start painting on the sidewalk or driveway!

vigorous—forceful

DISCOVER THE STARS

MATERIALS

printable constellation cards

paint or markers

empty toilet paper or paper towel tube

The night sky is full of stars that are millions of miles away. Scientists have linked some stars together to make *constellations*. With this project, you'll be able to look at the sky and find your favorite stars and constellations. You'll never look at the night sky the same way again.

1 With an adult's help, find a website with printable constellation cards. Or check out a book with maps of the constellations at the library. Study a few constellations, and find some favorites.

2 Using the paint or the markers, decorate the cardboard tube. This will be your pretend *telescope*. Longer tubes make better telescopes.

3 Using the constellation cards or book, choose a constellation to find in the sky.

constellation—a group of stars that forms a shape

telescope—a tool people use to look at objects in space; telescopes make objects in space look closer than they really are

TIP:

Cassiopeia is an easy one for starters. It looks like the letter W.

4 With an adult's supervision, go outside somewhere dark, such as a backyard or in the countryside. Close one eye and use the other to look through your new telescope. The telescope blocks unnecessary light and will help you focus on small parts of the sky, making it easier to see the constellations. How many constellations can you find?

PHOTO SAFARI

MATERIALS

a camera or cell phone with photo capability

a safe place to explore

computer and printer

glue

small 4 x 6-inch (10 x 15-centimeter) piece of cardboard

twigs or small branches

twine or string

Imagine you're an adventurer on a safari. All it takes is a camera and some ideas and you have an afternoon of outdoor fun. What will you choose for your safari topic? Wild animals? Creepy, crawly bugs? Challenge yourself and your friends with this photo safari! Meet up after the safari to compare your pictures.

TIP:
Try to pick a topic you enjoy and can find nearby.

1   Ask an adult's permission to use a camera or a cell phone with photo capability. If you don't know how to use the camera or phone, ask for instructions.

2   Choose a topic for your photo safari. You could try to find as many different kinds of birds, bugs, or animals as you can. Perhaps you prefer road signs or different types of trees.

3   With an adult's supervision, find a safe place where you can roam around and discover a variety of your topic targets.

4 Start taking pictures! Experiment with different angles and camera settings to create fun and interesting photos. Lie on your back to get a different view. Try out the *panoramic* setting on your camera for a wide shot.

5 While you're taking pictures, keep an eye out for twigs that you could use to make your picture frame.

6 Get together and look at all of your photos! Have each person pick out his or her favorite photo.

panorama—a wide or complete view of an area

7 Ask an adult to help you print your favorite picture.

8 Glue your photo onto the piece of cardboard.

9 Use the twigs and twine to create a decorative frame around the edge of the photo. Simply glue the pieces in place however you'd like. Now it's time to admire your new work of nature art!

GIVE THIS A TRY:
Challenge yourself or friends to see who can find 10 different items first. Or create bingo cards and make it a game!

NEIGHBORHOOD SCAVENGER HUNT

MATERIALS

pen and paper
a bucket or bag

When you're hunting for something to do, maybe it's a hunt that you need! A *scavenger hunt* is a game that gives you clues to find certain things. You'll have fun making a mad dash to find the things on your list. The list can be anything from random backyard items to different kinds of tree leaves. Compete with your friends to see who can finish first!

1 Create the scavenger hunt list. If you have multiple players, one person can be the judge and make the list. Or ask an adult to create one for you using items that can be found in the area where you will be playing.

2 The same person who made the list should also create clues to help you find the items. Clues are optional, but they make the game more fun and challenging.

3 Collect the items in a bag or bucket.

4 Be the first one to find all the items and win!

scavenger hunt—a game, typically played in an outdoor area, in which participants have to collect a number of random objects

Scaveng

☐ Heart-shaped

☐ Flat rock

☑ Pine cone

☐ Dandelion

☐ Lizard

☐ Fall

GIANT LAWN GAME

scissors

cardboard box

large roll of string

2 small stakes for string

4 cans of ground-marking spray paint in green, red, blue, and yellow

paper and pencil

What's more fun than playing a board game? Playing a life-sized board game on your lawn! This simple version of Twister can be created as big as you want so you can have any number of players.

TIP:

Do not use regular spray paint. This could kill the grass!

1 With an adult's help, cut a hole in the bottom of the cardboard box 6 inches (15 cm) in diameter.

2 Tie the string around one of the stakes. Push the stake into the ground. Stretch the string in the direction you would like to make your game board. Then tie the other end of the string to the other stake. Push the stake into the ground.

3 Using the string as a guide, make the first row of dots using one color of spray paint. Use the box as a stencil to create circles.

4 Repeat step 3 with the other colors of spray paint to make the game board. There should be one row of each color.

5 Wait a couple hours for the spray paint to dry.

6 Cut eight small pieces of paper. Each piece of paper should be labeled for a body part or color. For body parts, use: right hand, left hand, right foot, and left foot. For colors, use the four colors of your spray paint.

7 Invite some friends over to play this classic game!

NEVER PLAYED?
HERE ARE THE RULES:

Three to five people should stand on the game board. A "caller" draws two slips: one body part and one color. Then, he or she calls them out. For example, "Right hand, green!" Each player has to try to put his or her right hand on a green circle. Don't lose your balance!

RAINBOW BUBBLE SNAKES

MATERIALS

liquid dish soap

bowl

water

corn syrup (optional)

knife or scissors

plastic bottle

cotton washcloth or sock

rubber band

food coloring in multiple colors

Rainbow bubble snakes look like long, brightly colored serpents! They're easy to make, and your friends won't believe the amazing bubble snakes you can create.

TIP:

A little bit of the corn syrup can make your bubbles stronger, but it is not necessary.

1 Add 3 tablespoons (45 ml) of dish soap into a bowl. Then add 1 cup (240 ml) of water to the bowl. Stir the *solution* together. Let the bowl sit for a few hours.

2 With an adult's help, cut the bottom off the plastic bottle.

3 Place the washcloth or sock on the bottom of the bottle, completely covering the opening. Secure the cloth or sock to the bottle with the rubber band.

4 Place a few drops of food coloring on the cloth. Use several colors to cover the surface of the cloth or sock.

5 Dip the cloth end of the bottle into the bubble solution. Make sure the cloth gets completely soaked.

6 Blow through the drinking end of the bottle, and watch your rainbow bubble snakes appear! Who can create the longest snake?

solution—a mixture made of a substance that has been dissolved in another substance

GLOSSARY

constellation (kahn-stuh-LAY-shuhn)—a group of stars that forms a shape

grommet (GROM-it)—an eyelet placed in a hole of a tarp or panel to protect a rope or cable passing through it or to prevent the tarp or panel from being torn

panorama (pan-uh-RAM-uh)—a wide or complete view of an area

scavenger hunt (SKAV-uhnj-uhr HUHNT)—a game, typically played in an outdoor area, in which participants have to collect a number of random objects

solution (suh-LOO-shuhn)—a mixture made of a substance that has been dissolved in another substance

species (SPEE-sheez)—a group of plants or animals that share common characteristics

telescope (TEL-uh-skope)—a tool people use to look at objects in space; telescopes make objects in space look closer than they really are

vigorous (VIG-ur-uhss)—forceful

READ MORE

Isaac, Dawn. *101 Things for Kids to Do Outside*. Richmond Hill, Ontario: Firefly Books, 2016.

Kuskowski, Alex. *Cool Outdoor Activities: Great Things to Do in the Great Outdoors*. Cool Great Outdoors. Minneapolis, Minn: Abdo Publishing, 2016.

Ventura, Marne. *Cool Cardboard Projects You Can Create*. Imagine It, Build It. North Mankato, Minn.: Capstone Press, 2016.

INTERNET SITES

FactHound offers a safe, fun way to find Internet sites related to this book. All of the sites on FactHound have been researched by our staff.

Here's all you do:

Visit *www.facthound.com*

Type in this code: 9781515747031

Check out projects, games and lots more at
www.capstonekids.com

INDEX